Evening Shades of Grace

A book of prayers, blessings, and laments

by
George Phifer

Evening Shades of Grace

Copyright © 2013 George Phifer

Cover illustration © 2013 Veranne Hall Graham.
Used by permission.

Photograph by Abi Phifer

All rights reserved. No part of this book may be reproduced or transmitted in any form or by any means without written permission from the author.

ISBN: 978-1-937975-16-6

RNWC For His Glory
An imprint of
RNWC Media, LLC
PO Box 559
Pinehurst, TX 77362
www.RNWCMedia.com

Printed in USA

Dedication

This book is lovingly dedicated to my wife,
Charlcie Phifer.

A wonderful companion, friend and soul-mate who loved Jesus above all other loves and in His love found the love she needed to love her family, friends and others.

Her testimony was that she only thought she knew Jesus until she met Him. Life was never the same after that day, as she became a dangerously wonderful, Christ-like person. Graduating Summa Cum Laude in Pipe Organ, music was her life and love until Jesus put a new song in her heart. Combined with her God-given talent and that new song in her heart, she trained and encouraged many musicians, artists and worship leaders to lead many people in worship.

The song of joy and sorrow ran deep through her life, yet the singular, penetrating, dolce melody of Christ's love always rang clear and true. Her music and creativity lifted our hearts heavenward and deeply touched the longing in our hearts for something more,

more than this life has to offer – we will never be the same. Her influence and inspiration are the reason for the writing of this book of prayers, blessings, and laments.

Preface

More than likely, you and I have many things in common. We share good times and bad times, joys and sorrows. We share the experiences of life. As long as I can remember, I have been jotting down little expressions of my experiences of life in prayers, praises, blessings and laments. Some that I share are from my teenage years, some from the years I was courting my wife, and our lives together. Most are recent attempts to express and share the grief I have experienced in losing her.

When we married, we loved a popular song, "Celebrate The Whole of It," and we made that the theme of our lives. We have shared together many joys and many losses, including her mom's Alzheimer's, and the deaths of our parents, my brother and his wife, and many mentors and friends, and through each loss, we determined to celebrate the whole of it. When Charlcie, my wife, died suddenly right after Christmas 2011, it seemed the right side of my life was amputated, and the left side was shattered into a thousand little pieces. I had no idea how I would pick up the pieces, much less celebrate the whole of it. But by faith, I began to celebrate the grief I was experiencing, and one way of expressing this was in these musings.

About four years before this, I had been challenged by a friend, Darrell Harris, to do something with Facebook that might be helpful or add meaning to people's lives. I did this for two years, and then went through a very difficult time and stopped doing it. When Charlcie died, I was writing in my journal to help me process my grief. Someone suggested it might be therapeutic and helpful to others for me to share my journey through these short expressions.

Many of them had to be cleaned up, and many others I couldn't share, because they would be so shocking. It is my prayer that they will in some way inspire, comfort, and challenge you; that the manifold shades of God's grace will fill your evenings with His presence.

January

January 1

Lord, let our days add up to years of goodness and faithfulness. Post Steady Love and Good Faith as lookouts through the night.

January 2

Evening shades of Grace, cover us like a warm Comforter. Your glory, oh Lord, gives light through the night, Your mercy succors the hurting, and Your undying Love embraces the dying.

January 3

Lord, let the light of the last day fall on us tonight. Let the power of the age to come break through the darkness. Let the hope of new creation dawn on us as the shadows lengthen.

January 4

Lord, we travel light and celebrate the unfolding journey with thanksgiving; we lie down in peace and rise up with joy to sing Your praises.

January 5

El Dorado, the utopian dream is always around the corner, but never arriving. El Shaddai, Your Kingdom has arrived in Jesus, reality blossoming in the darkness and flourishing through suffering and death to resurrection life. Those who rest in You shall rise to praise Your Name.

January 6

Christus Victor, how foolish sounding is the message of the cross to those who live in the passing shadows of dusk. But to us who trust in You, it is the power of a New Day breaking in the fading dimness of the old one.

January 7

Lord, all our fear knots that turn our lives into frayed knots are resolved by Your "Fear not for I have redeemed you, I have called you by name, you are mine! Fear not little flock for it is your Father's good pleasure to give you the kingdom." Lord, we trust in You to untie the fear knots tonight so we can get some rest.

January 8

As our prayers rise to You, let Your peace fall on us and calm our minds to hear You, open the eyes of our hearts to see You. Fill our dreams with praise and thanksgiving as we rest in peace.

January 9

Awesome God, wipe away every tear, drive out every fear, still the noise. Let us drink in the silence. Quietly now, ever so quietly sing... ever so gently sing, whispers of love, echoes of mercy.

January 10

From evening to evening Your justice is more evident, but few take notice. Quietly, so quietly we go about Your business. Wake us to serve the poor, feed the hungry, care for the widows and orphans, visit the prisoners and pray for the sick.

January 11

Great Joy, O Lord, seems too often to go hand in hand with Frightful Sorrow. But still the Joy is worth the Sorrow - if indeed they go together. If there is a choice of one without the other in some safe middle way, we choose the heights and the depths together. Lord have mercy on us tonight.

January 12

A sudden Grace Incarnate, crying love, love is the only way through the shadows. A sudden Glory and Love, dear Love, arose from the depths of darkness. Desperate dawns our Living Hope.

January 13

Glorious in Holiness, Fearful in Praises, Doing Wonders, the only Wise GOD. Plural in Mystery, without One there is NONE, No One. No ONE is like YOU. We rest assured.

January 14

Lord, tonight we choose the obedience that is our freedom, for in Your chains is perfect liberty. Gladly we obey of our own choosing. Your service is our emancipation, our joy and our rest.

January 15

Incarnate God, who created the world and suffered it to crucify You, have mercy on us tonight. We ask not for earthly gain or worldly pleasure or hidden treasure but for the least, the last and the lost. Lord have mercy, Christ have mercy, let mercy triumph over judgment.

January 16

O Joy that breaks our heart with longing, O Grace that draws us ever homeward, O Mercy that reveals the Love of our desire, the only real Love, we take our rest in You until we arrive at home.

January 17

Many sorrows cannot quell Your Presence, darkness cannot quench Your Light, and death cannot quash Your Love. May Your Presence be nearer, Your Light burn brighter and Your Love be stronger in the darkness tonight.

January 18

The chilling edge of night crawls over the sunset and with dreadful ease slays the sun. Yet in the darkness, stars shine bright, singing evening songs and hymns written in the Light that warm our souls until the dawn that never ends.

January 19

Red velvet sunset fades into shadow; the evening deepens and silence reigns. Quiet our hearts and stay our thoughts; still the noise till we hear whispers of love and echoes of mercy, and our souls find rest in You!

January 20

High heaven and earth below, praise the High King of heaven who stooped so low. Sun, moon and stars, all you dust dwellers, you morning stars shining in the deepest darkest night, praise Him. Praise the High King of Heaven.

January 21

The sun lavishes dusk with brilliant hues and delicate shadows, and just beyond lie evening shades of grace and rest. We open our hands in thanksgiving, and our lips sing hymns of grateful benedictions, as our eyes close in restful sleep.

January 22

Sometimes, Lord, the darkness descends so deeply we can barely remember the Light. Give us eyes to see the Light shines still, and let us rest in the Light of the future tonight.

January 23

YOUR "I-ness", Holy unspeakable four-letter Word, only once have You revealed YOUR Name, "I AM," who YOU are in YOURSELF, the unbelievable absolute act of being. YOU created us in YOUR image, and we are "I's" because YOU are "I AM." Give us eyes to see YOU tonight and rest in being. (Idea from Peter Kreeft, *Between Heaven and Hell,* IVP Books.)

January 24

Lord, in the solitude of evening, in the still of the night, silence the dark voices and quiet our own destructive chatter, for it is in solitude we are alone with You and in silence that we will hear Your voice and find rest.

January 25

We lift our eyes to You in the night watches; as musicians look to the hand of their conductor, as racers running the race look for the flag, so our eyes look to You from start to finish.

January 26

The joy of our salvation was like a dream come true, like living water in the desert, like a thanksgiving feast. We laughed and danced and sang songs of joy. Tonight, Lord, come again and bring the rains to our drought-stricken lives, to those who sow in tears, so those who go out, sowing seeds of salvation in distress, will sing and dance and laugh again, will celebrate the feast until You come again with all the saints.

January 27

Lord, the scepter of the Dark Knight rests on the just and the unjust alike. But his rule doesn't go unchallenged, for the Morning Star has already arisen and signs of the New Dawn are already on the horizon. Not yet has the darkness passed, but already the Light is shining.

January 28

Shouts of joy resound in the tent of the undeserving, and mercy echoes in the chambers of our hearts. You set our tent on solid ground. You mended our broken hearts and You will clothe us in a new tent when we break camp.

January 29

Lord, we are but a breath, a flickering flame in the wind. Our days are like passing shadows. But You have lit our hearts with an eternal flame and You will clothe us with embodied life. May we burn bright, so the lost can find their way home.

January 30

May our evening prayers rise before You like sweet incense, the lifting of our hands as sweet surrender. As we kneel in humility and bow our hearts and heads with gratitude, Lord, fill our hearts with thanksgiving, and may our lips offer sacrifices of praise.

January 31

The wet chill of winter bit our lips and frosted our eyes tonight, Lord. But nothing can dampen our praises or blind our eyes to Your beauty. Be near and warm us, wrap us in Your Comforter and open the eyes of our hearts as we rest in You.

February

February 1

Mighty Lord, give the tongue of worries the axe and make them split; head off troubles with one swing, that we might find rest tonight.

February 2

When the unspeakable happens Lord, we realize we must grieve and suffer to rebuild a meaningful life. It can't be avoided; there's no other way out but forward, into the abyss, setting us on a journey, whether we were ready or not. But You have made the journey and know the way. Take our hand and lead us through the valley of the shadow of death.

February 3

Tonight, Lord, we pray: teach us to seek justice, encourage the oppressed and defend the fatherless. Help us plead the cause of widows and single moms and lift up the working poor. Tonight, Lord, we pray for Your mercy.

February 4

Lord, we were born on the wrong side of the tracks and our lives were like tar paper shacks on a dead end street. Until You came to live on the wrong side of the tracks, we had no hope. But You took us in, gave us a roof over our heads and sent us back out to the wrong side of the tracks. Now we live on the right side of tracks in the wrong side of the tracks 'til You come again! Make it quick, Lord.

February 5

Lord, You are our Mighty Warrior King who rules through the cross. You give us healing through wounding, salvation through suffering and resurrection through death. The one-way street to dead end, You changed into a You-turn, too.

February 6

Lord, we are drowned in deep pools of anguish, shocked to death by lightning-quick troubles and cut to pieces with sharp stabs of pain. Come rescue the wounded, bereaved, and dying tonight. Lord, be near, within reach, and dry the tears.

February 7

Lord, we have drunk the winsome wine of the age and eaten the bewitching bread of this generation. We have become thin and weak, empty suits without substance. You offered us New Wine of the Age to Come and the bread of tomorrow, the Substance of the world to come, Light in the night. But we refused. We rush toward a dead end street and don't even know it. Forgive us. Lord, have mercy. In Your kindness we will find repentance.

February 8

Lord, when we spread out our hands in evening prayers, do not hide Your face from us; don't close Your ears.

February 9

The Stars curtsy and the moon bows as they begin the evening dance. The Cherubim cry "worthy, worthy, worthy" as the Seraphim echo back in antiphonal response "is the Lamb that was slain." All creation joins in the chorus of hallelujahs, and the night winds play flute and piccolo in rising worship.

February 10

Let our praises place You center stage. Like a telescope, let them enlarge Your reality and cause everything else to diminish. May praise be our occupation and Your love our preoccupation until we wake up in the New Day to come.

February 11

Lord, we are like ancient oaks with fading leaves and weakening limbs; we are like a mighty city with crumbling walls and waning foundations, magnificent ruins. Re-form the ancient foundations and renew the magnificent oaks in our day, Oh Lord, in our day.

February 12

Lord, every bone in our body is singing Your praises. Every fiber of our being is laughing, because You scare the pants off troubles all day long. Cares ain't got a chance to steal our sleep. Whew -- we can't save the world -- You already did it!

February 13

All the poor and powerless are here to worship; those who never get their acts together are here, too. We took You at Your Word, with simple trust, and rest on Your Promise. Oh for Grace to trust You more.

February 14

We lift our hearts before You; we sing and adore you, for You alone are Holy. You have filled us with joy. Your glory fills this place. Your wonder fills this place. We lift our hearts before You, Lord!

February 15

Lord, we are marked people, citizens of the baptismal city. The are-nots of this world and the have-nots, reduced to nothing, dying with You. Yet we are Your chosen image-bearers, part of Your Kingdom come and coming, rising with You. May we rest in peace.

February 16

Lord, we kneel beside our bed to stand in Your presence; we bow our heads to hear Your voice. We close our eyes to open the eyes of our hearts; we lift our voices to sing Your praises and raise our hands with thanksgiving. With all our being, we love You.

February 17

From frost's first kiss, a winter's chill has set in that seems to have frozen time. Buried beneath the ice-covered ground, a seed lies silently, waiting, waiting Love's first kiss of Spring. Oh Lord, help us endure the long winter's night; let the light of the New Day shine on us tonight.

February 18

Anxieties sound like animals that howl in the night. Worries taunt us like broken records. But only a whisper of praise to You, God of Mercy, only an offering of thanks silences their taunts and sends them howling, fading into the darkness.

February 19

Lord, You are a shade from the heat of the day and a flaming fire from the cold of night. You are a shelter, a hiding place and a refuge from stormy nights and rainy days. You are home to us for the rest of our lives and when we wake we'll see Your face.

February 20

Help wanted, watch repairers, no experience necessary. Look out for the lost, restore the wounded, repair the broken, unwind the wound up and renew the weary. Lift up your eyes and look on the field--no time to waste.

February 21

Lord, instead of the apron of humility, we dress in fine linen. Sackcloth and ashes should be our dress and a towel to wash each other's feet should be our preoccupation. Pierce our ears and brand our hearts to claim us as Your own. Make us Your servants Lord; make us Your wait-people.

February 22

The best time of the day is the night time. The best place to be is with You. The best thing to see is the moon and stars and wandering stars reflecting back Your glory. The best songs are evening vespers and the best prayer is Your Kingdom come on earth as it as in heaven. The best bedtime story is the Good News: the Morning Star has risen in the deepest darkest night to signal the New Dawn coming. The best rest ever is in Your Grace.

February 23

From the beginning of the street to the end, on the corner of first and last, we'll hold a street meeting for the least, the last, and the lost. From A to Z we'll fill the air with salvation songs.

February 24

Ribbons of color harmonize across the sky, a symphony in red, nature's crescendo. There is wonder in every sunset, a beauty that comforts us. Just beyond lies evening Grace and rest.

February 25

In the night when we cry out, You hear us and make us bold. You give us strength in our hearts and cover us in the darkness. When we rise, You throw off the covers and robe us in glory.

February 26

Your voice, oh, Lord, oh, Your sweet gentle voice whispers 'peace' in the chaos of our lives, and echoes of mercy stay our troublesome thoughts and still our souls that we may find rest. Sing, Lord, sing over us tonight songs of comfort and cheer.

February 27

Lord, as the shadows lengthen and the darkness grows, let the light of the age to come break through to our hearts and minds. Let the hope of new creation rise in our souls and give our bodies deep rest 'til the New Day dawns.

February 28

Holy ONE, Holy, Holy, Holy, Only ONE, Father, Spirit and Son. Plural in Majesty, Majestic in Holiness and Wholly Other - The ONE GOD, Community of life-giving Love, shared in sacrificial love, brings us to our knees in surrender to Your Holy Love.

February 29

God of wonders, what a glorious night! The moon beams the music of the heavens, and the stars relay the melody in whisper-like beauty. The wind chimes in such perfect harmonies underneath, behind, and around the tune, and all creation hums along for the rest of the night.

March 1

How lovely to behold the bright Morning Star, risen in our darkest hour, shining the way to the New Age dawning. What Comfort in our sorrow, what Joy in our sadness, what Light in the dark night of our souls. Oh, how lovely to BEHOLD!

March 2

Lord, we have ruined Your vineyard, plundered the poor, and crushed the orphans, grinding the faces of abandoned and forgotten youth into the ground. How long, oh Lord, how long will You put up with us? How long does mercy last? Your mercies never come to an end.

March 3

Kindle a burning like the burning of a fire in our bellies, oh Lord. Passion for Jesus and comPassion for others to be our ComPass through the night. So light a fire in Your people, oh Lord, and a flame to devour the Dark Knight and burn up the darkness.

March 4

Lord, we are children given to corruption; we have forsaken You and turned our backs. But not You, Lord, You have never forsaken us or turned Your back, and You never will. Your discipline and even Your silence is tough Love. And when You say "no" You mean that is the answer, "No!" Help us trust what we just can't understand.

March 5

Now unto the King, Eternal Father, Immortal Son, Invisible Spirit, the only wise God, be glory and honor forever. Speak wisdom to us through the language of dreams and restore us through the night.

March 6

Lord, You encamp round about us, You have pitched Your tent among us, and You inhabit our praises. You sing, Lord, You sing over us songs of deliverance and weave garlands of the never-ending love of Jesus as our crowns, and You festoon mercy and grace to drape over our lives. Oh, what a wonderful, wonderful Savior You are!

March 7

Being Beyond Imagination, Surpassing Comprehension, Numinous Communion, Blessed Trinity! You are Great-hearted in grace, lavish in love and matchless in mercy. Tonight we bow before You in stunned silence at Your awe-full presence in our lives.

March 8

Lord, troubles are near; evil surrounds us like a herd of bulls. El Toro is pawing the dirt; nostrils are flaring; horns are lowered ready to charge. Rescue us; snatch us from the horns of a dilemma. You are the only escape. We look for You in the watches of the night.

March 9

Lord, hear our prayer tonight; keep us from the haste of impetuous, forgetful delight and the quickness of impulsive thoughtlessness. Let us live with the patient power of knowing You go before us, and we can trust in You.

March 10

In the quiet of the evening, in the stillness of the night, Mercy whispers our name, forgiveness echoes faintly in the distance, calling us home, calling us to dare to draw near the One who loves us most.

March 11

Almighty God, You make the boogeyman pull the covers over his head; his fiends hide under the bed. We have nothing to fear: not angels or demons, seen or unseen powers, not even death. You alone are fearsome. You are awe-full and we rest in You!

March 12

As the late evening sun slips through the window tonight, let our hearts slip into Your presence. Let our prayers be a fragrant aroma before You and our praises a sweet-smelling incense. Let Your blessing rest on us and calm our hearts to rest in You.

March 13

O Desire of our souls, with our whole hearts we have longed for You in the night watches. By Your Spirit within, we will seek You early and often. Let grace and mercy be shown to the lost and Your favor to Your people. Lord, You are a crown of glory and a diadem of beauty to those You have rescued. Amazing Love You are.

March 14

Troubles will thrive and terminate, worries will wax and wane, and sin will surge and shrink, but our relationship with Jesus is eternal, never-changing, never-ending. We can always rejoice, whether in good or bad times, bright or dark, because they are temporary, and You are permanent.

March 15

Lord, give us the grace of perseverance. Like blind Bartimaeus, may we fight our way through the darkness and shout our way into Your presence and cry out for Your mercy. Give us ears to hear Your call and jump to our feet with the joyous jubilation and reckless response of a soul suddenly welcomed by the King.

March 16

Lord, hold us together tonight, because we're coming apart at the seams. Seems like heartaches are our constant diet; seems like tears are all we have to drink. Seems like You're so far away, that it seems like You're not around. Seems like what is evident isn't always what it seems like.

March 17

Only One, Father, Spirit, and Son. Only You are worthy of our praise. Only You we adore. Only You give rest and life evermore, Only One.

March 18

Keep a positive outlook and your nose stuck in the book, your eyes focused on Him. Then your heart will begin to rise above the trials and your prayers will fill a beautiful perfume vial. They will begin to minister refreshment when the seal is rent, and the ointment releases the tantalizing fragrance of a broken life.

March 19

Your mysterious love, oh Lord, is fierce enough to penetrate the loneliest night. The echo of Your infinite Mercy amplifies the gentle whisper, "I Am here. Rest in Me."

March 20

Lord, we weep with grief as deep as the ocean's depth. Encourage us with Your Word. Give us peace that passes all understanding, as we cling to Your presence.

March 21

Your presence, Lord, is better than strawberries in the Spring; Your kindness than peaches and cream. Your Word is better than the best comfort food, and You are home to us for the rest of our life.

March 22

Oh, give thanks to the King of Heaven, who stooped down to rescue us from the Dark Knight. You became dust to make us just. Oh, give thanks to the King of Heaven.

March 23

Lord, we've finally found a place to lay our heads, a place we can find peace and quiet. We haven't anything to contribute but a weary soul and a heavy heart. We've finally found a place to hang our hats, in Your presence, Oh Lord.

March 24

Lord, late into the evening we keep company with You. We open our hearts to You and hold nothing back. Tears flood our bed and sorrows wash over us. Be near to those in danger, care for the sick and dying, and catch the falling.

March 25

Law courts and legislatures, centers of banking and commerce, temples and capitals: places of power wielded to the benefit of the already powerful and the trampling of the already powerless. Beware; the tables will be turned on you. What's done in the dark shall be brought into the light, for the present order of darkness is being replaced with the light of God's new order.

March 26

Lord, as we turn in for the night, let praise be our evening sacrifice, let thanksgiving be our fragrant offering, and let our prayers be kindling to light a fire in our hearts.

March 27

Lord, many of us have not the strength to mount up with wings as eagles; others have not the legs or breath to run and not grow weary. We walk with a limp and can only muster the strength to walk and not faint and that only by Your Grace. Steady us when we stumble, catch us when we crumble, and wait with us when we're too weary to take another step. Renew our strength as we rest in You.

March 28

Even though there be no cattle on a thousand hills, no oil in the ground or the Gulf, no fruit in the Valley and cotton balls lie rotten; yet we will rejoice in the Lord! Soul! Be joyful in the Lord of your salvation. The Lord is your strength, even in your weakness and dullness of awareness of His Presence. He will make you like a longhorn, sturdy and stable, and bring you through the desert places. Like a whitetail deer, He'll bring you safely through the hill country. Soul, rejoice in the Lord! (based on Hab. 3:17-19).

March 29

Awe-full Presence, awe-struck Wonder, awe-sum total of all Love; we bow our heads and kneel our hearts before You. We bend our knees at the foot of Your cross, the joy set before You, the ransomed of the Lord, slaves set free.

March 30

Resurrection, this side of Sunday tears shoot from our eyes, grief overwhelms our souls tonight as we contemplate so many loved ones fallen asleep in Christ. Death seems so permanent and so unforgiving this side of Sunday. Oh, how the disciples must have despaired that Friday and Saturday. We would, too, if it weren't for Sunday. Sunday changed everything. Living Hope, we trust in You!

March 31

Give God a standing ovation as the curtain falls tonight! Sing praises to the tune of His glory and set thanksgiving to the rhythm of His blessing. We never stop enjoying Your Name and fame.

April 1

Unbutton your lips and let loose with shouts of praise; put on your dancing shoes, kick up your heels, and dance the night away; act the part of a fool, a fool for Christ. The joke is on the devil; death was hoodwinked and the grave left empty. The King of Glory rules. He has the last laugh!

April 2

Rein in the storms, Lord, hold back waves of evil, and restrain troubles tonight. We give you full reign, Lord. You stepped into the darkness and reign in the light. Hope blossomed in the dead of night, flourished through suffering, and was vindicated in the resurrection. Rain down Your power and might on us tonight.

April 3

Mighty and splendid is the King! Lift up a shout of praise, dance with all your might, raise your hands and clap for joy. The risen King is among us. Let us bow down and worship Him together; all together now sing songs of celebration; all together Rock the house. Mighty and splendid is the Risen King!

April 4

Majesty, You are higher than anything and anyone, outshining the moon and the brightest stars. None can compare with Your glory. You scoop up the poor from the dirt and rescue the outcasts thrown out with the trash. None can compare with You.

April 5

As we lie down for the night, worries tune up and anxieties strike a dissonant chord. The Dark Knight whispers harmonious disquiet and devils chime in. But Your praises, Oh Lord, silence our foes. Praise disbands the instruments that rob our sleep and keeps beat with God's heart until we come to rest.

April 6

The deeper Your Love, Oh Lord, the higher it goes. The wider Your Mercy, the straighter we become. The sounder Your Word, the more quiet rest we get.

April 7

As the evening deepens Lord, You have done many good things for us that we hardly even notice. Give us thankful hearts. Forgive us for noticing the few troubles and worrying more than praising. Give us a peaceful end and wake us with joy unspeakable!

April 8

Let us cry to the Lord our God. Now is the time to mourn and lament, to weep with those who weep, nurse the brokenhearted and comfort the grieving. Mend our broken hearts tonight and stand guard over us, Lord. Sing songs of comfort over us and cover us with Your unfailing Love.

April 9

Lord, guard us from self-talk, disguised as harmless sheep, but really wolves that tear us apart. Protect us from poison darts sent to contaminate our dreams, and extinguish flaming arrows meant to wound our hopes.

April 10

Oh, to speak with stammering lips and to sing with voice so weak the Holy Name of Jesus. Just to whisper the glories of Your Name calms my heart to rest in You and causes my ears to hear You, my Faithful Friend, my Comforter. Only You can mend my broken heart.

April 11

Lord, life has a way of grinding us like wheat and crushing us like grapes. Make us bread and wine for the world, filled with Your presence. Even as bread and wine must rest in the making, make us rest in You.

April 12

Lord, it's a good thing we stumbled on You and fell on the Rock, because we would never get up if we didn't.

April 13

Let all that is within me cry Holy, Holy, Holy is the Lord. Let every fiber of my being worship Your Grace. For You have come to us on Your terms. You Love us as we are and not as we should be. All Is Grace. Oh Lord, help us grasp this tonight.

April 14

Lord, from once upon a time to Kingdom come, You have always been the best bedtime story. Whisper words of blessing that echo in our hearts until the dawn of a new DAY.

April 15

Your faithfulness, Lord, will see us through the night. Surprise us with Your love at daybreak; put a skip in our step and a dance in our feet all day long.

April 16

Our defenses are down and our lives are shaken and splitting open. Seal the cracks and reinforce the beams, before we completely collapse in the darkness. Mighty God, be our defense, restore us to Your favor, and give us grace and mercy tonight.

April 17

Steal away with Me tonight; steal a moment, an hour, an evening. Steel your thoughts with MY promises; steel your soul with MY Word. Still your heart and enter the quiet. Be still and know that 'I AM' Your GOD. Steal away with Me tonight and rest.

April 18

As the twilight turns to darkness, we sing songs of such sorrow, laments for a world gone wrong. Be merciful, oh Lord of Mercy, and let Your light shine brighter in the darkness tonight.

April 19

In the stillness of waiting, Lord, let our silence become a time of listening for the prayers the Spirit is praying, wordless groans deep within. Let our souls find rest, cradled in Your arms.

April 20

Tonight, Lord, we come to You with a sense of our own spiritual poverty; we don't fully even know what we need. We come with empty hands and empty hearts to receive what it is You have for us, for You know what we need. Come give us rest; we trust in You.

April 21

Lord, calm the storms to a whisper and still the waves to a ripple. Bring us safely into harbor and cause us to rest in Your faithful love.

April 22

Lord, there are moments our souls long just to be with You; we thirst for Your presence and hunger for You comfort. Make the moments longer and more often and show us the way to our heart's deepest Desire.

April 23

Lord, we're in the State of Fragmentation. We are frenetic doings not human beings. We just can't seem to unplug. We are exhausted by the constant intrusion and overstimulation of technology into a soul-numbing sadness. Breaks in the day are filled with texts, phone calls, emails, tweets and just noise. How can we hear You, when we can't even hear ourselves or anyone else? What's that? Come away with You to a quiet place and don't bring my phone? Isn't that a bit extreme? Lord, have mercy on us!

April 24

In the beauty of silence, the beyond-words-place, we listen for the prayer that's already being prayed. With voiceless groanings and soundless sighs, we enter into prayers for the hurting, needs of others, the sick and dying, and we wait with them in Your presence, Oh Lord.

April 25

When longings stir in the quiet of the night, Oh Lord, and we become painfully aware of our brokenness, and hunger for real change growls within us, may we embrace the moment and not turn away. May we ever be turning and returning to You, our only Hope and Promise.

April 26

Wholly God, our souls are holey, shot full of holes. Make us whole. Holy God, we are wholly sinners; make us holy. Holy, Holy, Wholly God, make us wholly holy in Your Grace.

April 27

Lord, when longings ambush us with a ferocity that stops us dead in our tracks, a longing for love that takes us by complete surprise, we are acutely aware of our brokenness and amazed that underneath the noise of our busy lives lie such tender longings. It brings us to tears in humble gratitude.

April 28

Lord, thanks for tastes of eternity, moments where our longing for You is satisfied, and we enter into the timelessness that is You. We are lost in Love. Yet those moments bring painful awareness of our separation from You, and we try to do everything to numb the pain and escape the angst, instead of just resting in You. But, oh, are those moments worth it! May they be more and last longer and help us rest in You between the times.

April 29

Lord, be with those of us who grieve deeply our losses tonight; shed tears of sorrow with us; sit with us with our questions and attend to our loneliness. Not everything can be fixed or solved, so be near and dear to us in that place of quiet agony and do what only You can do, for from You alone comes our salvation.

April 30

Lord, You make broken, discarded, and cracked pots into valuable vessels. Paint us works of art and color us reflections of Your Light and Glory. We are servants of Your Grace and vessels of Your Honor.

May

May 1

Sadness and Sorrow, my twin friends, have you come to sit with me again? Through the dark night watches and the wee hours of the morn, never the silence broken but, oh, the words you've spoken. Grievous words of lost love and dreams and longing for what's gone, but also for the One whose words can heal the soul's deep longing and give us bright hope for tomorrow.

May 2

I spy! Lord, You're hidden in plain sight. Open the eyes of our hearts to see You. Quiet our souls long enough to hear and see the clues You give. Silence the noise within, so we can enter a time of quiet alertness and stillness, to find You in the midst of it all. Are we getting warmer?

May 3

Lord, without time for joy, time is meaningless. Without time for pleasure, time is empty. Without time for rest, time has no rhyme or rhythm. Without time for tears, time has no comfort and compassion. Lord, without time for You, time is vacuous. Lord, time is short. Help us make the most it.

May 4

As we lie down, guard us as the apple of Your eye. Hide us in the shadow of Your wings. Protect us from wicked thoughts that attack us, from murderous condemnation that surrounds us. They track us down and throw us to the ground. Arise, Mighty God, and stand against them and bring them to their knees.

May 5

Before it ALL – Holy, Holy, Holy LOVE; first and last of All, Suffering Love; through it All, Faithful Love; after it All, Endless Love. Most of all, I love You because You're YOU - Amazing LOVE!

May 6

Lord, when we're chronically apprehensive, our thoughts create bogus threats, worrying beyond imagination. We don't need lions, or wolves, or dark nights to frighten the daylight out of us. We rest in You and find peace in Your presence.

May 7

Lord, in this dark and dismal hour, we are wandering around in tears and sorrow. With heavy hearts, we grieve the passing of dear friends. Gone! Absent, decamped -- now camped out with you on a nearby hill we can't get to ... yet! No longer will we hear their laughter or feel their touch. Suddenly dreams are over and plans undone and we are left chasing normal, if there be such a place.

May 8

Lord, fill our ears with songs of praise, still our minds with words of peace, delight our hearts with pictures of hope, and close our eyes with visions of grace.

May 9

Lord, our eyes shine with joy, and our hearts reflect the radiance of Your glory. As the moon and stars in deep darkness reflect the sun, so Your people shine Your love like sunburst brightness for all to see.

May 10

In the stillness of your soul, in the quiet of the night, in the deafening silence, you'll hear a quiet whisper, and when you linger long enough, you'll detect the distant echo, "You are my chosen one, my special child, my beloved. Sit here with Me, and out of this place of rest will come strength for the day."

May 11

At day's end, draw us into Your holy rest. Let us join in quiet communion and find peace in Your presence.

May 12

Comforter, multiply our rest to us and refresh Your weary people. Then we will flourish like the leaves in spring, blossom like fruit trees, and produce fruit, drawing strength from You.

May 13

Grief, Lord, is like speaking an unknown language, foreign to those who can't know the depths of our pain. But You, oh Lord, interpret our sighs and groanings. You know the language of grief, inside and out. Help us, Lord, to find rest tonight.

May 14

Lord, You sent help from heaven; unfailing Love and Faithfulness have come to see us through the violent storms. Worries like whirlwinds twist everything out of proportion, and troubles like tornadoes spin things out of control. But You hold us in Your hands and never let go.

May 15

Immense Mercy, Immeasurable Love, Immensurable Presence: God without measure, we give You unbounded praises, jaw-dropping awe, and eye-popping wonder, from the break of day 'til the setting sun and right on through the night.

May 16

Lord, every Spring You send us flowers, every evening a gorgeous sunset, and every morning a magnificent sunrise. Whenever we want to talk, You listen, when we're in trouble, You help, and when we're confused, You understand. You can live anywhere in or outside the universe, and yet You choose our lives. How amazing is that!

May 17

Lord, we're running to You as fast as we can, but it feels like we're losing ground. It's a good thing we begin at the end, start at the finish line, because we would never make it any other way.

May 18

Holy Comforter, come alongside the heavy-laden tonight, and lift off the heaviness that weighs us down. Strengthen us in the inner person to stand and cry out for the hurting, the sick and the dying. Empower us to release Your Kingdom and give us the lost; fill us with songs overflowing with praise.

May 19

Died in the Wool Savior, Hope woven into the fabric of our lives, unchanging Love, and Grace that never fades, hold us fast through the night and make us steadfast to the end.

May 20

Oh, to whisper with quivering lips and stammering tongue Your merciful Name, "Jesus." Just to breathe out the glories of Your lovingkindness, my faithful friend, brings comfort to our souls. Tears stream down our faces and flood our pillows; only You can mend this broken heart.

May 21

Deliverer, make trouble be a stranger to us and cause grace to be our friend. Make evil avoid us and sorrow neglect us. Let mercy surround us like the arms of a friend and whisper blessings over us while we sleep.

May 22

At times, Lord, our prayers dribble down our chin. In total despair we abandon ourselves at Your feet. A silent scream bursts from our lips. We are spent, done, fresh out of words, but You still read our lips. You still hear our groans. We are the prayer tonight.

May 23

Lord, we are only here a moment, aliens and strangers in a fallen world system, as our ancestors before us. Our time on earth is like a shadow, gone so soon without a trace. But You, oh Lord, are our home. You have pitched Your tent with us for the night and given us an everlasting resting place.

May 24

Emanuelle, Present absence, Sorrow of Heart has moved in and her twin sisters, Anguish and Grief of Soul, followed with her. But You are well acquainted with them. As our older brother, Future Hope, You came before and have gone ahead, leaving Your Comforter to move us into Father's house, where we await Your return.

May 25

Worries drain our strength, troubles conspire against us, and temptations set traps to snare us. But You, Oh Lord, are our strength. You watch over us and spring traps. We can rest easy in Your unfailing love.

May 26

Evening Bread, we are a broken communion in a broken world. Gather the broken pieces to do Your work. Give us the bread of tomorrow today, so we can feed the hungry, help the hurting, and bring justice to the poor.

May 27

LORD, don't hide from us tonight! Desperately our heart whispers, "seek God" and our whole being echoes back "I am, amm, ammmm." Don't let the Dark Knight hide YOUR Love from us.

May 28

In the darkness that haunts me, its silent whispers taunt me; yet deeper still sounds the voice of Love. Light overflows the dawn, rolling back the darkness, and now I'm living safe in the clear and resting in songs of mercy.

May 29

Troubles boil faster than a pot on an open flame; condemnation brews caldrons of evil. Before what they cook up is half-done, Lord Almighty, throw it out with the garbage. Fill our hearts with praise, seasoned with thanksgiving, until it boils over into a peaceful night.

May 30

Lord, we are but lighted signs, pointing the way in the dark to the distant horizon. We're not photographs of what may lie beyond, but roadside markers, pointing the direction home. Don't let the power run low and our lights flicker and dim.

May 31

As our prayers rise to You, let Your peace fall on us and calm our minds to hear You. Open the eyes of our hearts to see You. Fill our dreams with praise and thanksgiving.

June

June 1

Prince of Peace, anxious thoughts stand speechless before You; things that go bump in the night flee Your Presence. Keep us in perfect peace as we sleep. Wrest all the cares from our hearts, while we rest in peace.

June 2

Toss out the bad eggs, condemn the condemners, and trouble the troublemakers. Shout and give thanks and sing the blues away with praise.

June 3

No more tears, Lord, no more pain—no more sorrows and no more troubles, for our loved one is present with You. We give out heart cries to You, Oh Lord, our HOPE. Tears roll down our faces like mountain streams in the Spring, and joy fills our hearts with quiet rest.

June 4

Your forgiveness, Oh Lord, puts us on the road to Life. Your signposts are clear, and Your caution lights give warning. Your love directs us to Hidden Treasure, and Your Grace pays all the travel expenses.

June 5

Oh Lord, what a glorious night. The evening sings Your praises, and the stars chime in. Giant Blue Spruce wave thunderous applause, and the Rocky Mountains do homage. The winds whistle in tune, and all creation calls Your Name. You alone are God!

June 6

Lord, troubles and trials have a way of grinding us like wheat; worry and woes have a way of crushing us like grapes. Make us bread for the hungry and drink for the thirsty. Give us the apron of humility to serve the poor and care for the sick, and may we be life-giving communion to the dying.

June 7

Lord of Hosts, all the saints on earth and in heaven praise You! Death and sickness still resist, but lose ground, as Your Kingdom comes on earth, as it is in heaven. We long for the day when those who weep no longer weep, the sick are well, and there is no dying. Let it be tonight!

June 8

Creeps hide in the shadows to trick us; Bully tries to intimidate and whisper accusations in our ears. But God laughs; they're all bad jokes without a punch line, clowns without costumes. When He puts on the lights, they vanish into thin air, and the forgiven receive rest that lasts forever.

June 9

Be still before the Lord; quiet down and listen. Cool your pipes, bridle your tongue, and trash the rubbish. God doesn't lose any sleep. He's not bedeviled with trepidations or bewildered with troubles, and neither should we be. QUIET!

June 10

ALONE, You ALONE have saved us. Give hope to the hopeless and life to the lifeless. You ALONE walk with the lonely through deep sorrows, with the solitary through dark shadows. You ALONE will never leave us or forsake us.

June 11

Lord, You're not impressed with atomic power. The size of our nuclear arsenal or military power won't save us. But those who are God AweFull afraid get His attention and His power and might to see us through to the end and beyond.

June 12

High heaven and earth below praise the High King of heaven, who stooped so low. Sun, moon and stars, all you dust dwellers, you morning stars shining in the deepest darkest night, praise Him! Praise the High King of Heaven!

June 13

Evening sea breeze gently sings, darkness deepens to a hush, and your soul is still within. Listen, listen with your heart. You can almost hear Him calling, calling you home, calling you to come into the quiet for the rest of your life.

June 14

Lord, have mercy on us tonight. We close our eyes to see You, bow our heads to hear You, and bend our knees to stand before You. We serve You to know such freedom few have ever known.

June 15

From evening to evening, our prayers come before You as a sweet smelling aroma. In the stillness of the night, our praises rise like a warm and fragrant incense. Let Your presence rest on us and calm our hearts to rest in You.

June 16

Your Grace, as we lie down tonight, please bring comfort to the comfortless, give succor to the hurting, mercy to those who deserve none, and let Your loving-kindness surround us with quiet peace and calm our hearts to rest deeply in you.

June 17

Lamb of God, slain but Conquering, conquer our fears tonight, slay our worries, and cast down our anxieties. Send the boogieman packing, so we can hit the sack and rest in peace.

June 18

Sing praise songs to the ever present Messiah and tell His story to everyone you meet. He goes out in the night to track us down and dogs our trail, searching for us to bring us back alive. He keeps His eye on us and registers every whimper and moan. We're never alone.

June 19

From East to West and dusk to dawn and back again, keep shouting your praises to God. Just to speak His Name is praise, and troubles tremble. Just to remember the Son drives the shadows away. Bless Him now, tomorrow and always.

June 20

The end of the long night is assured, and we are secured in Your love, but we are not safe in the darkness. Guard us, Oh Lord, and walk with us through the valley of the shadow of death. Lead us to a peaceful end.

June 21

God of creation, You hung the moon and flung the stars in place, like a giant mobile hangs over a baby's crib. You set the planets in orbit and wrote praise graffiti across the evening skies: Orion, The Pleiades, Leo the Lion, and Ursa Major, the Great Bear. All creation declares Your glory, God of Creation.

June 22

Oh Lord, how lovely is the evening. The moon sings songs of sheer delight, the stars hymns of joy, and the wandering stars burst into psalms of praise. All the heavens serenade us with words of Your love that calm our hearts and give rest to our souls.

June 23

Mourning by mourning new mercies we receive: Your steadfast love never ceases to cheer us; Your faithfulness endures through the night, and Your Grace leads us to joy in the morning and Hope eternal.

June 24

Lord, we mourn with loud lamentations tonight and weep bitterly with deep groanings, until You set us free. Constant is our pain, but so are You.

June 25

Lord, as darkness creeps in, we always run straight to Your arms. So why would we run anywhere else, when the doomsayers cry that the bottom has dropped out and we ain't got a chance? You never head for the hills. Your address never changes, and we always have a safe place to lay our heads.

June 26

Shut the lying lips of temptations. Silence the voice of condemnations and the mumblings of worries. Make love and faithfulness our occupation and Your love and faithfulness for us our preoccupation for the rest of our lives.

June 27

Lord, we are torn and ragged nets in Your hands; mend our brokenness. Cast us where You will, for we can't cast ourselves. Use us to draw many to Your Kingdom, for we rest in Your hands.

June 28

Lord, as we turn in tonight, turn our cares into prayers, our worries into calmness. We toss and turn out our troubles with thanksgivings, and praises drown out anxious thoughts.

June 29

In the quiet evening, the solitude of stillness, when we are alone with our prayers and our hearts open to You, encourage us with Your word and restore us through the night.

June 30

Carpenter, hammer, and nails saved our lives, and now with hammer and nails You're building us a home with You for the rest of our lives. Thanks for the rest.

July

July 1

Golden Orb, setting in Hill country splendor, splashing sunset colors all across the heavens. Evening's shadow stretches across the lake and settles round us like a warm embrace. The beauty of this moment fills our souls with rest and quietly, ever so quietly, we hear You calling us home.

July 2

Living Hope, we're like shadows in the campfire, puffs of smoke that fade into the night. We're migrant workers just passing through. Show us the way; take us by the hand for the rest of our lives. You alone are our hope and portion.

July 3

Your path, Oh Lord, would we travel; our own would we refuse. When we lie down and when we rise up, when we travel through the valley of the shadow of death, and when we reach the mountaintop, Your path, Oh Lord, would we travel.

July 4

Found Hope, that was never lost, but I sure was. Living Hope, rolling back the darkness like a bonfire burning brighter, offering Resurrection light. Future Hope, shining like a lighthouse on the darkest stormy night, promising us safe harbor, and Present Hope, captaining the ship all the way until we reach home.

July 5

The sacrifices of praise, oh Lord, are a work of heart. Their words have still their ancient power to calm our soul and give rest to the weary.

July 6

Lord, we need all the light we can get, but, oh, how we need fire! We need the gentle rains of refreshing, but, oh, how we need thunder and lightning! We need the wind and the whirlwind. Set us aflame and put thunder in our voices and wind in our sails. The still, small voices of widows and orphans, single moms and their children, the sick and the poor are going unheard while Your people are indolent, preoccupied with every agenda but Yours. We need a people like our Founding Fathers who pledge life, fortune and sacred honor for freedom and justice. Once again, Lord, the authority of establishment must give way to authority of witness, suffering servants committed to a revolution of kindness, living with less, to give more and overthrow the powers of injustice.

July 7

Keep watch with us tonight, Lord. Weep with those who weep, care for the dying, and comfort the grieving. Stand guard and sing songs of deliverance over us. Cover us with Your unfailing love.

July 8

Like stealthy shadows, vain imaginations creep in, condemnations lurk about the gloom, and worries slink in like shades of doom. But in the Light of Your Love, they vanish into thin air, and Your beloved find rest that lasts forever.

July 9

Tonight, Lord, as we withdraw into silence, bring to us quiet alertness. Our deep desire is that You would meet us and whisper specifically in our hearts Your love and acceptance. Create a space where we share Your Presence.

July 10

Lord, as the day fades into night, let our last waking thoughts be praise. Cover us with Your love, watch over our sleeping, and wake us with a kiss, oh Prince of Peace.

July 11

Lord, You grant power and position to serve others, so we fall on our knees and faces as our position to receive Your power for the powerless, to wash feet, feed the hungry, clothe the naked, protect the defenseless, set the captives free, care for widows and orphans, nurse the sick and watch over the dying. Lord, to do all that, we better stay on our faces day and night.

July 12

Creator, in those twilight moments between waking and sleeping, Your wonders are too numerous to count. Words fail to express Your glory and are too few to account for You. Our last waking thoughts are praise and thanksgiving.

July 13

Dusk and dawn take turns calling: come and worship, worship the Maker of heaven and earth. All through the night watches, make thanksgiving your habitation and when you rise, make praise your offering and obedience your prayer.

July 14

Without Your Grace, what protection do we have in the darkest night? Everywhere we look is corruption and undoing. Evil Tsunami rises ever higher. But You, oh Lord, rise higher still, as Tsunami waves pass away. Hide us in the shadow of Your wings tonight, and may we rest in peace.

July 15

Oh, how our hearts thrill at Your manifest presence; how every fiber of our being comes to attention and the hair on the back of our head bristles! You are here with us in the night watches.

July 16

Those who camp out in Your love, oh Lord, are like Zion Mountain; nothing can move it. Your presence is rock solid. Even death, like darkness, can't penetrate the light You surround us in. When we break camp, You will take us home.

July 17

Now Here, we are lost in Your presence and are free from endless and fruitless bouts of self-pity. Here we are found in the ubiquity of the eternal NOW; in this moment, we find the rest of our lives.

July 18

Your Word, Lord, is settled forever, and Your throne is unshakable. The glory of Your Kingdom power is disposed towards us. Promise shines from Your throne and gives us hope through the night. An open door gives us access to Your presence.

July 19

Who would have thought salvation would look like this: suffering LOVE! Who would have thought of God becoming sin for us, saving us through weakness, forgiveness through death, and life through resurrection? Who would have ever thought? Only You, Oh Lord, only You, and we can rest deeply on that.

July 20

AweFull Presence, when we wake in the middle of the night, tears shoot from our eyes, and violent sobs wrack our bodies with the ache of an awful absence. We are comforted, O Lord, with Your AweFull Presence. Hair-raising and eye-popping Wonder, give us peace of mind.

July 21

Humble King, You haven't ignored the plight of the needy. You didn't turn and walk away. You listened to our cries for help and walked right into the fight. When they thought You were down and out, and night had won the day, new creation sprang to light in the darkness and grows ever brighter.

July 22

Lord, when troubles come, conceal us in Your hand; hide us in Your shadow. You never promised we wouldn't have troubles, just to guide us personally through the thick of them.

July 23

Oh Lord, God of all comforts, had You not suffered, how could You help us in our suffering? Had You not been wounded, how could You heal our wounds? Had You not died, how could You be with the dying? Had You not overcome, how could You grant us to overcome? Lord, tonight we pray, give us courage that dares and fortitude that endures and patience that overcomes, O Lord, God of all comforts.

July 24

O Love revealed at Calvary, Your glory lights the way through the night and reveals that something amazing happened, that something shows You are the Messiah, that the age to come has broken into the present and shines through the darkness to the New Day breaking. O Love revealed in Resurrection Life.

July 25

Oil Lamp, burn bright: olive berries, bruised and crushed beyond all semblance of berries. Oil, beaten out for the light, cause our lamp to burn all through the dark night and beyond. Living Flame, Word A-Fire, You are a Lamp for our feet and Light for our path.

July 26

"We must through much tribulation enter into the Kingdom of God" is not a fair weather word, O Lord. Yet we think it strange, unreasonable, or unjust when storms and floods, trials and troubles, sorrows and suffering come upon us. We've been given abundant life but not leave to steal quietly to heaven without conflict or cross.

July 27

Lord of Grace, we can find treasure where it may be hidden, even by moonlight. Any who walk in difficult places, who care to, may gather those treasures and lie down without fear and rest in peace.

July 28

O Love that has led us all our life long, we rest our hearts upon what we know and leave what we do not in Your hands. O Love that has given all Your life, all Your life long, we lie down in Your love and rise up in Your life.

July 29

Lord, Your glory is on display in the sunset skies, Your handiwork splashed across the horizon. Vesper songs fade, their voices not recorded, but their silence fills the earth with praise.

July 30

O Joy that has led o'er hill and dale, through vale of tears to mountains of delight, sunny slopes and cloudy ravines, You give Living Hope, reasons upon reasons for resurrection life and not one for fear. Oh Lord who casts out all fear, we rest in You.

July 31

Lord, our heart and our soul fail; our portion has been stolen. Be Thou the strength of our heart and soul and our portion forever. Give us rest, oh Lord, give us rest.

August

August 1

Lord, because of Your kindness, we will look You in the eye. We will rise up and see Your fullness and live heaven on earth.

August 2

Ours, Oh Lord, is the ordination of the pierced Hands, the ministry of the towel and basin. Our cup, Lord, is the cross, our crown, resurrection life. A cup full of sorrow, when shaken, cannot but spill drops of comfort. Oh Lord of the cross, hold us so close that we are drawn into that fellowship, that thirst, then pour us out as a drink offering for the least, the last and the lost. Let this be our crown, Oh Lord of the cross.

August 3

Your courageous Love, Oh Lord, is brave enough to trust us to endure, not fearing the Dark Knight. We keep on going as ones seeing "Him who is Invisible" and Your Grace lights the way for us through the darkness in triumph.

August 4

Lord, give us a peaceful end that is the beginning of what never ends. Surround us with songs of deliverance, and let mercy rule in our hearts.

August 5

Grief, Lord, is the cost of loving someone, and, oh, how You love us. Your undying Love gives grace to the lost and hope to the hurting and unending life to the dying.

August 6

Your love, Oh Lord, with all its agonizing possibilities, did not desire for us the less costly love which shrinks from the supreme demand. Your divine love You desired should be in us, the love You loved us with, with all its agonizing possibilities - but with joy set before us as a sure-fire inevitability as we pass through the flames.

August 7

After a shadowy day, Lord, we look for the moonflower to open in the dusk. We watch it unfurl its wide-open bell, a coronet of wonder. In the beauty of the evening, may our hearts unfurl in wide-open praises, a crown of wonder to Your Grace, as the shadows fade from our souls.

August 8

God of Mercy, watch with those who wake, be with those who weep, nurse the sick, rest the weary, comfort the dying, shield Your joyous ones, and all for love's sake.

August 9

Yesterday, oh Lord, is a cashed check; tomorrow is a promissory note, but today we are change in Your pocket. Spend us well.

August 10

King! Your reign outlasts the sun, outlives the moon. It's like rain on dry ground and life-refreshing showers of mercy. Let kindness burst into blossom, and peace abound until Dawn fades to dusk, sunset turns to sunrise. Age after age, You reign!

August 11

Tonight, Lord, we thank you for the empty promise of resurrection: empty tomb, empty graveclothes, and empty graveyards. Resurrection deflates worries, runs anxieties out of gas, and frees us from empty threats and accusations. You unpacked our burdens, emptied every care, and You give us the rest of our lives.

August 12

Lord, fill our ears with songs of praise, still our minds with words of peace, delight our hearts with pictures of hope, and close our eyes with visions of grace.

August 13

Lord, the moment we arrive at Your door, we're never sorry we knocked. You're a safe-house for the storm-weary, and the second we enter, we find rest for our souls.

August 14

Lord, You track down temptations and trap them in the very traps they set. You've got Your eye on us, and Your ear registers every moan and groan. Don't let anything rob us of sleep tonight.

August 15

Close our eyes in slumber; open the eyes of our hearts in wonder. Dazzle our dreams with streaming videos of Your presence, coming into the present.

August 16

At day's end, Lord, we're ready for sleep. We rest in You, until the break of day, when we rise to meet You face to face.

August 17

Watchman, watch the One who has bound the evil one; keep your eyes on the One who causes us to come to life. Keep your eyes on the One who reigns over all powers and calls us to join Him through the night watches.

August 18

Jesus, You corralled all our sin and gentled the wild horse in our hearts. You chased all the howling wolves of worry into the night and called us to warm ourselves at Your fire. In You we find rest for the night.

August 19

Oh Lord, our Lord, how great and awesome You are. Wrapped in evening glory, the lights of the night acknowledge Your beauty. You blanket our lives with lovingkindness and cover us with Your faithfulness. In You alone do we find rest, our perfect end.

August 20

Oh Lord, what a glorious night. The evening sings Your praises and the stars chime in. Ocean waves thunderous applause, and night creatures roar their approval. The winds whistle in tune, and all creation praises You. You alone are God!

August 21

Beyond-among-us, Emmanuel, here and still beyond anything we can think or imagine, watch over us and be near to us. As terrifyingly comforting as that is, we can only whisper the prayer of the tax collector: "Lord, be merciful to me, a sinner."

August 22

Lord, for fear of losing face, we get out the cosmetic kit and put on our virtuous face. We hide our brokenness behind superficial happiness and spend sleepless nights worrying someone will see through our masquerade. But the face we fear losing is the mask of the imposter, not our own. Lord, have mercy on us sinners.

August 23

Lord, as the evening sun slips through the window, how we long to slip into Your presence. You are with us in the faces of the poor, in worship, and through word and sacrament. Your hidden presence by Your Spirit is only a hint of the real meeting to come at the end of the Day.

August 24

In the quiet of the evening, in the stillness of the night, Mercy whispers our name; forgiveness echoes faintly in the distance, calling us home, calling us to dare to draw near the One who loves us most.

August 25

Lord, let evening grace find us trusting in You. Help us go into the night blessed with dreams, possibilities and promises of the New Day. Quiet our souls, console the inconsolable, and be near to all.

August 26

Evening Grace, we bow our hearts to You and pray; we bend our knees in grateful gratitude. We thank you for shelter and rest, for love and joy, and for friends and family.

August 27

Lord, tonight our hearts swell, yes, even burst with delight. Our eyes shine with a twinkle of Your light, and our souls thrill with great rejoicing for those in exile. The discarded, unwanted, unloved, and marginalized return, preaching the praises of Your might love and acceptance.

August 28

In Jesus we find the tears of God poured out; only the suffering God can heal the brokenhearted. Your holy tears, Lord, lead to our liberation from sorrow and victory over death. You come to lead us through the night to the joy that comes in the morning. You have already entered into the new morning of resurrection, while we groan, eagerly awaiting the new day dawning.

August 29

Lord, when life feels more like a death march through the night than a ticker tape parade in the day, we look to You. Gethsemane, the worst day of Your life—but the end of the story is never disappointing. You marched through the night of death, disarmed the dark powers through the cross, and paraded their weakness in the light of New Day. Lord, the end of our story will never be disappointing, no matter how dark the night.

August 30

Trials and trouble, Oh Lord, appear to be the hammer and chisel of Your Grace, as You sculpt something more beautiful than we can imagine out of the warp and woof of our lives. We are but clay that rests in Your hands.

August 31

Lord, tonight we don't feel like singing, so we sing anyway. We sing of Your majesty and power, of Your presence in our lives. Fears flee and troubles fade as we are lifted up on the wings of a song, for You, Oh Lord, give songs in the night.

September

September 1

As we follow the Man of Sorrows, the Resurrected King, we come out of the night into the light, out of our loss into gain, out of our pain into peace, and out of our bitterness into forgiveness. As we come to Him, our labors cease, and we find rest.

September 2

From the dungeon of despair, at the midnight hour, we sing songs of praise. The foundations of despair are shaken, the locked doors of discouragement fling open, and the chains of fear are loosed. Sing, Lord, sing with us songs of praise and bring a new dawn of faith.

September 3

Hot tears burn down our cheeks, and heavy sobs convulse our bodies, as the only outlet for the pain that has seized our souls tonight. Thank you, Lord, for faith to weep openly and uncontrollably, for the Word becoming flesh that You, Oh Lord, might join us in our tears for the rest of our lives. *(Based on 1 Samuel 30:4, when David and his mighty men wept until they had no strength left over the capture of their families at Ziklag.)*

September 4

At eve's end our prayers long for You to speak, as flowers long for the rain. We wait eagerly for Your words, gracelets as refreshing as a summer shower. Renew us in our rest tonight.

September 5

Listen, Oh Lord, to the anguish in our hearts tonight. Turn to us; we can't wait. Be near to the grieving, care for the dying, and dry the tears of the hurting. Calm our hearts to hear You and open our eyes to see You, for You are enough.

September 6

Blessed Lord, we kneel before You with hearts full of thanks; we bow our hearts and our heads, crying out, "Lord have mercy on us tonight."

September 7

Here I Am tonight, standing in your midst. Here I Am, a man of sorrows, with you in every sorrow. Here I Am, a present help in times of trouble. Here I Am to give rest to the weary. I Am here.

September 8

Shepherd, watch over Your sheep tonight; tend to the young lambs. Wolves take one look at you and run away, with their tails tucked between their legs.

September 9

Mend our broken hearts tonight, Lord; put us together with all Your skill. We long to see Your finished product.

September 10

The songs we sing in the dark, oh Lord, beside the rivers of exile, reveal what's in our hearts. We sing the song of Moses and the song of the Lamb, because when our Passover Lamb was slain, the Lord became our salvation. Great and marvelous are Your deeds, indeed!

September 11

Oh Lord, too often we focus on the exceptional and forget Your Spirit keeps the Sun in orbit, the circuit of the moon and stars in place, and sustains all creation with wakefulness and rest. Open our eyes tonight to see the Spirit makes the world go round, not just see the miraculous surprises.

September 12

Lord, let the light of the Last Day fall on the night and light our way to a peaceful end.

September 13

Lord, have mercy on us. Compulsions push on us, bothers attack us all day long, and fretfulness hounds us to death. But when we are ill at ease, sick and tired, we put our trust in You, and You put us at ease.

September 14

Lord, we are arrogantly indifferent to You, until we get into trouble. Don't be indifferent to us and give us what we deserve. Instead, we pray for mercy and forgiveness tonight.

September 15

Oh Lord, our shield, guard us from annoying attacks that are like vicious snarling dogs that want to chew us up and spit us out. They come out at night and try to rob us of sleep, but they go away unsatisfied, oh Lord, our Shield.

September 16

Dusk to dusk, evening to evening, one day at a time, we trust in Your amazing love. As the morning star rises in the darkest part of the night, so You, our Morning Star, have risen in our darkness, revealing Your love, and will be with us through the rest of our lives.

September 17

Lord, let our praise throw a spotlight on You in the darkness. Let it be like a fire in the night, a beacon for the lost to find their way, a place to warm ourselves and rest in safety.

September 18

One and only, we wait for You silently in the darkness. We are empty and void, lighter than a puff of air and weigh less than nothing. Speak life, new creation, and give us breathing room before our last gasp. Silently we wait, for You are our One and only.

September 19

Our defenses are down, and our lives are shaken and splitting open. Seal the cracks and reinforce the beams, before we completely collapse in the darkness. Mighty God, be our defense, restore us to Your favor, and give us grace and mercy tonight.

September 20

Lord, we're chasing Daylight into dark places, going into the unfamiliar and unexplored, letting go of safety, and switching certainty for trust in You.

September 21

Lord, many lives are in chaos and darkness. You haven't gone mute, so speak a Genesis week into the empty and destitute. Let there be light, new creation, people shining like stars in the night.

September 22

Lord, we've thrown our lot in with You tonight. You went out on a limb for us and came through alive. We will always trust in You.

September 23

Humble King, You put on the apron of humility. Wash away the dust of the day, all our anxieties and the cares we wear, that sleeping, we might rest deeply and waking, we may walk in Your ways, Lord, refreshed.

September 24

How strong is Your love, Oh Lord. We find refuge in the shadow of Your wings. You fill us with good things, and we drink from the streams of Your delight. For with You is the source of life; by Your light, we see light, and by Your presence we find rest.

September 25

Evening Grace, let Your blessing fall on us. May the vesper lights find their voice and sing over us through the night.

September 26

While we sleep, tune our hearts to Your frequency. Dial in Your signal and drown out every anxious thought. Break through the jamming devices with blessings and songs of deliverance.

September 27

Come, fellow travelers, and stand in the wind. Come for refreshing and come for new life. Holy Wind, breathe new life into Your people; inhabit our praises and drown out taunting worries. Holy Wind, blow.

September 28

May God the Father give us peace tonight, and God the Son pour out His love into our hearts, helping us cry "Abba, Father." And may God the Spirit give us rest and comfort, and may the One God cover us with grace.

September 29

Father, have mercy on us, sinners redeemed by Your grace; Christ have mercy on us, sinners forgiven by Your sacrifice; Spirit have mercy on us, sinners enlivened by the same power that raised Christ from the dead. Merciful ONE, we rest in Your salvation.

September 30

Mighty God, guard our dreams and protect us from fears that trouble us. Tread underfoot all our cares and captivate us with thoughts of You.

October

October 1

Rock Solid Shelter, cover us with Your Comforter and sing songs of mercy over us. Whisper peace in our hearts and smile on us with blessing tonight.

October 2

Mighty God, You strong arm the strongman, tie up the boogeyman and turn him into a frayed knot. You take captive every anxious thought and bring peace to our hearts and hope to our dreams.

October 3

Good Shepherd, guide us in the light and in the dark; stand guard over our sleeping, walk sentry around our hearts, and keep us in perfect peace.

October 4

Lord, we thank you to the tune of Your faithfulness. We break out in song with a lung full of praise. All night long we're singing about You and Your wonders.

October 5

Who can stand before You, Mighty God? Darkness is scared stiff. The Dark Knight seethes in rebellion, running for the shadows. You stand against all who do evil and have come to rescue the oppressed.

October 6

Sunset colors blaze across the evening sky, evening quiet descends all around us, and the moon and stars silently sing your praises. Open our eyes to see the beauty all around us, open our ears to hear the vesper songs, and teach us to pause and be filled with wonder tonight, Lord, tonight.

October 7

Man of Sorrows, acquainted with grief, Suffering Father, Holy Comforter, the only wise God, comfort the grieving tonight, blanket our minds with Your peace that passes all understanding, cover our hearts with Your promises, give rest to our weary souls.

October 8

Wave Runner, calm the storm on the seas and in our minds; Wind Rider, tame the winds that beat upon the rocks and on our hearts. Whisper peace in a still small voice, and sing songs of love that echo in our minds through the night.

October 9

Awesome One, we bow our heads in thanksgiving tonight. We kneel our hearts in praise, for You give rest to the weary and calm the anxious storms.

October 10

At the end of the day, Lord, it's Your love that gives us a sense of meaning. Your faithfulness shapes us and defines us and shows us the way we should go. When we miss a step or get lost in the darkness, we can rest assured Your love will light the way ahead.

October 11

We love You, Lord, and thank You for the rest we have tonight. Help us unwind, body, mind, and heart, and prepare us for the new day coming. Living Hope, lighten the weight of darkness, lessen the pressure of burdens, and diminish the density of disillusionment. Fill us with expectation to rise abiding in You.

October 12

Your Word, Lord, is settled forever, and Your throne is unshakable. The glory of Your Kingdom power is disposed towards us. Promise shines from Your throne and gives us hope through the night. An open door gives us access to Your presence.

October 13

Director, show us Your unfailing mercy on the big screen of our dreams, cover us with compassion, and grant us rest for our weary souls.

October 14

Lord, we can't control events, let alone whether we'll make it through this night. So our prayer tonight is simply "Let Your Kingdom come on earth as it is in heaven." Give us the bread of tomorrow today.

October 15

Let praise echo in the chambers of our hearts through the night, send waves of mercy to subdue our troubles, and give us rest.

October 16

Night Watchman, sound the alarm! Panic attacks and fear surround us with the terror by night. But You, oh Lord, are our defense, praise is our shield, and You hide us under the shadow of Your wings.

October 17

Suffering Lord, hear our anguished cries. Our pillows are soaked with tears; we can barely catch a breath between sobs. Praise dribbles down our chin -- oh God, oh God, oh God -- let this bitter cup pass from us. You conquered death, and it must submit. Give life to our loved ones.

October 18

Lord, can we bend Your ear here for a moment tonight? Times of trouble are stalking many people, but You are a present help through it all. Be near to the hurting, as only one hurt as bad as You can, and care for the dying, as only one who has been raised from the dead can.

October 19

Artist in Residence, You paint the night with hope. The works of Your hands praise You all day long. Evening sings songs of thanksgiving to Your Name. The quiet of the night shouts, and deafening silence stills our souls in awe.

October 20

King of heaven's armies, immense and august in Your humility, You put arrogant oceans of condemnations in their place, and You calm unruly waves of anxiety. You gave the big bully the boot, and brushed off our enemies like fleas off a wet dog.

October 21

Lord, many times we are but an echo of our enemies' behavior, not a people who bless those who hurt us. Tonight, Lord, make us an echo of Your Love, a reverberation (repercussion) of Your grace and mercy.

October 22

Night Watchman, watch with those who serve tonight: soldiers on duty and in harms way, wait staff, police officers, firemen, cooks, EMT's, nurses, doctors, and all others. Watch with those who keep vigil through the long night for loved ones. Watch over us all.

October 23

God of Grace and Mercy, we're in over our heads. Open to us the springs of Your mercy, flood us with Your grace, and let the streams of Your kindness run through us.

October 24

El Shaddai, Your mighty hand frees us from hidden traps and shields us from deadly hazards. Your praise fends off worries, and thanksgiving drives troubles away.

October 25

High King of all, in one hand You hold the ocean depths, and in the other the moon and stars. Your hand sculpted it all and flung it in its place. The heavens sing Your praise, and the depths echo back.

October 26

Your faithfulness, Lord, will see us through the night. Surprise us with Your love at daybreak; put a skip in our step and a dance in our feet all day long.

October 27

In the dead of night, Calamity pounds on our Door and wails ominously at us. He draws his sword to strike, but You snap it in two like a toothpick. In Your house, Lord, no weapon formed against us can get past the Door.

October 28

Oh, how our hearts thrill at Your manifest presence; how every fiber of our being comes to attention, and the hair on the back of our head bristles. You are here with us in the night watches.

October 29

Your love, Lord, is the song we sing, telling all of your mercy. Your love is our foundation, and your faithfulness the roof overhead. It's the Comforter we sleep under.

October 30

Lord, all creation rejoices in Your wonderful ways. Choirs of angels sing of Your faithfulness. The moon and stars dance the night away. Search as much as we may, there's no one quite like You.

October 31

Lion Tamer, silence the roaring lions that prowl around, seeking to devour us. Trample troubles; strengthen the arms of the feeble and knees of the weak. Care for the wounds of the warriors; come alongside the ones we love. Be near to those far from us.

November

November 1

God of Glory, the path to glory is marked with suffering and service. Slave of all, we bow our hearts before You, and close our eyes in rest, that we may rise to serve with You and share Your glory.

November 2

High King of Heaven, guard us through the night; chase away the wolves that prowl on the edge of our dreams and let our anxious thoughts, like howling dogs, run away with their tails tucked between their legs. Be our refuge.

November 3

Lord, as night descends, we rejoice in You. We cast all our cares on You; let them slip from our hearts with prayers and thanksgivings. Strengthen us with rest, that we might serve the least, the last, and the lost.

November 4

Lord, quiet our hearts and silence our thoughts; kindle in us a fire of Your love to light our way through the night.

November 5

In the quiet of the evening, calm our hearts to be at rest. In our prayers we yearn to hear You gently speak that we belong to You.

November 6

Eternal King, unseen One who ever lives to show us mercy, You alone are God, and You watch over us with love and kindness. In the quiet of night, you cause our hearts to be at rest.

November 7

At day's end, draw us into Your holy rest. Let us join in quiet communion and find peace in Your presence.

November 8

Lord, we lie down in deep distress; we can't eat for sighing and our groans pour out like water. Evil lurks in the shadows of the Dark Knight, and their taunts pierce us like fiery darts. They scoff at our weakness. Yet in weakness, You overcame the Knight of Darkness to give us light to make it through. Our hope is in You alone.

November 9

Lord, You've put our feet on a wonderful road and taken us to a great place of rest. You've clothed us with the garments of praise and warmed us from the night chill with Your Comforter.

November 10

Life-Giving Word, tell us a bedtime story. Slay the evil dragons breathing fire down our necks, and vanquish our foes who rob us of much needed rest. Defend the defenseless and give rest to the weary. Cover us with Your blessings.

November 11

Lord, outrace our racing thoughts; bring them to a quiet end. Lift the burdens from our hearts and cover us with Your blessing tonight.

November 12

Night is falling, praise is rising, thanksgiving fills our hearts for helping us through the day. Whether joy or sorrow, troubles or not, You are with us; You are with us to the end. Be with us through the night and when we wake.

November 13

Almighty God, give our enemies the shakes all night long. Let their meal be bait in the trap that snaps shut; give the boogeyman a black eye, so we can get some shuteye.

November 14

As the evening fades, the day turns into memory. Let Your unfailing love cover our many failures. You suffer all our sins, and Your forgiveness is never ending. It doesn't seem enough, but all I can say is "thanks," and rest in Your arms of mercy.

November 15

Your grace, Lord, is our greatest treasure, Your love our greatest pleasure, and Your forgiveness our greatest measure. In You alone do we find abundant rest for our souls and a home for our hearts.

November 16

As the sun turns in for the night, and one by one the evening stars light, we thank You for a taste of things to come, a fragrance of things not seen, and signs of what will be, a new day dawning. As we turn in tonight, Lord, we find rest in Your Grace.

November 17

Like swarming bees, anxious thoughts hemmed us in; like wild prairie fire, worries pushed us to the edge. Restless and sleepless nights nearly did us in, when You grabbed us. Your hand turned the tide. Your hand held us together. Your hand, oh Lord, covered us.

November 18

From the rising of the sun to the end of night, Your Name, oh Lord, is praised! While we sleep, thanksgivings never cease, and when we wake, they increase. Blessed be the Name of the Lord!

November 19

Oh Lord, may all who seek You, find You, and be filled with joy and gladness. Remove the blinders from our eyes and the plugs from our ears that we may see Your face, and hear Your voice, and it will be enough.

November 20

I'm talking praise all through the day and thanks all through the night. And when we wake, let thanks be in our heart and praise on our lips.

November 21

Lord, troubles are like towering waves in the dark; we don't see them coming, but one minute we're up, and the next the bottom falls out. Our hearts get stuck in our throats, and we're spun around like a top. We called to You, and You quieted the wind with a whisper, harnessed the waves, and brought us back to safe harbor.

November 22

Great and terrible is Your beauty, Oh Lord. You give worries the willies, and temptations fall into their own traps, but You lay to rest those who marvel in amazement.

November 23

Jesus, You corralled all our sin and broke the wild horse in our hearts. You chased all the wolves into the night and called us to warm ourselves at Your fire.

November 24

You who watch by night, lift up your hands and bless the LORD. You who are weary, fill your hearts with praises that the peace of Christ may quiet your soul and give you rest.

November 25

Lord, troubles try and besiege us, worries bewilder us, and anxious thoughts betray us. But Your shield of strength is behind us, Your grace beneath us, Your Living Hope before us, and Your Presence always beside us. Nothing can touch us but Your love.

November 26

Lord, tonight, as we prepare for Thanksgiving, what have we to give to You: a cornucopia of sin, bountiful debts, wounds and hurts, and brokenness--our whole life, for You! How amazing is Your grace, how great is our thanks.

November 27

Rejoice in festal garments of praise; celebrate the meal to God with thanksgivings. Our God has blessed, is blessing, and will bless us in all we love and in all our work, so make a day of it.

November 28

Oh, give thanks to the King of Heaven, who stooped down to rescue us from the Dark Knight. You became earth to give us new birth. Oh, give thanks to the King of Heaven!

November 29

Great is the King of glory! Though You are Lord on high, You notice the lowly and give us rest.

November 30

In the night when we cry out, You hear us and make us bold. You give us strength in our hearts and cover us in the darkness. When we rise, You throw off the covers and robe us in glory.

December

December 1

Amazing Wonder, beyond all comprehension, You made Yourself known to us. Your mercy endures forever. You made the sun to rule the day and the moon and stars the night. Your favor is without end.

December 2

Many evenings we think we've loved You well, Lord. But Your heart whispers, "Love Me with all your heart, mind, and strength," and we must confess our love is diluted fruit of disordered and misdirected desire, made tasteless and flat by our lesser loyalties and divided hearts. Give us a pure and undivided heart, Lord.

December 3

Suffering Servant, You suffer the insufferable. You show mercy to the merciless and forgiveness to those who thumb their nose in Your face. What an amazing God You are! The very thought of You brings rest to my soul.

December 4

Temptations hunt us like a lion hunts in the dark, ready to pounce at the slightest opportunity. We rest secure in Your camp, where You keep vigil until the new day breaks.

December 5

Lord, as the day comes to a close, we stop and come to You. We've looked for the old, godly ways to walk in. We've traveled its path; now let us rest in You.

December 6

As the sun fades into the moonlight, we are reminded of light and dusk, clarity and mystery in the play of glow and shadow, an invitation to glimpse Your wonder and mystery. You, Oh Lord, delight in our search and desire, in making known and in hiddenness. Help us experience Your quiet presence tonight, and let the light of the age to come cast down the shadows that haunt us.

December 7

Great is the Lord, greater than our troubles, greater than our anxieties, greater than our fears, greater than our sin. Greater than all things that rob our sleep. We rest in You.

December 8

Father, watch over us tonight. Let the peace of Christ rule in our hearts, and send Your Holy Spirit to surround us with songs of salvation.

December 9

At the end of the day, Lord, You are a welcoming refuge and a strong fortress. The night watchman might as well take a nap.

December 10

Prince of Peace, anxious thoughts stand speechless before You. Things that go bump in the night flee Your arrival. Keep us in perfect peace as we sleep.

December 11

Unbutton your lips and let loose with shouts of praise! Put on your dancing shoes, kick up your heels and dance the night away! The King of Glory rules!

December 12

Almighty God, give us rest; wrest our cares, stress and anxieties from our heart and minds, and give us peaceful sleep. We cast all our cares on You, for You care for us. Surround us with songs of deliverance!

December 13

Lord, in the silence of the night, quiet our hearts and thoughts. Let the cares of the day wear off, and fill our hearts with thanks and praise throughout the night. Let us rise with prayers on our lips.

December 14

Come, Lord, scatter our vain imaginations, and blow away our fantasies like smoke in the wind. Silence our thoughts and in the emptiness speak life; fill our hearts with gratitude and our lips with praise all through the night.

December 15

Lord, when we lie down, don't let the swamp be our bed, the whirlpool suck us down, or the black hole swallow us. Let us sink into Your peace. Blanket us with your love; tuck us in Your arms secure.

December 16

Lord, we sing ourselves into your presence, and enter with the password "thankyou." We make ourselves at home in Your rest tonight.

December 17

Lord, create a moment of quiet within the clamor of troubles. Be our hideout tonight, our high mountain retreat.

December 18

Look in on us through the night, Lord. Station watchmen at the threshold of our dreams, and allow only good visions to enter. Turn away all cares and troubles. Thank You, Jesus!

December 19

High King, Creator of the earth, stoop down from heaven and wash the spiritual dust from our hearts, that we might rest deeply in Your love.

December 20

Lord, as we ride the wings of the evening into dreams, You place Your hand of blessing on us. Your strength will support us, and when we rise up, Your hand will be there to guide us.

December 21

Rising Hope, lift our hearts tonight. Future Grace, give us the bread of tomorrow tonight, and Certain Love draw us through the darkness into the light.

December 22

Oh Lord, we wait and watch for You, like sentries in the night. We long for You more than they long for the dawn. With You, Lord, there is hope and unfailing love; with You, Lord, we have a prayer.

December 23

Lord, turn our lives into a Bethlehem night, reveal Your present, and transform the ordinary into the extraordinary, like You did a feed trough into a manger.

December 24

Creator God, as I wander, I wonder. I wonder at the stars shining in the night, and I wonder at the moon that rules over the tides. I wonder that You have bowed much lower than we have fallen, so we can find rest for our souls. God of wonders, we bless You tonight.

December 25

Sing, Lord, sing over us with songs of deliverance, as we sleep. Troubles will flee before You, with worries close behind. When You whisper blessings, they run away like whipped dogs.

December 26

Burden Bearer, we come to You at the end of the day. Some are full of joy, and some full of sorrow. We are burdened with the cares of the world, and we care for the burdened of the world. Take our burdens, lift the weight off our shoulders, and give us rest.

December 27

Rescue us from our trials, Lord, for we hide ourselves under the shadow of Your wings. Cover us with Your lovingkindness, and wake us with new mercies every morning.

December 28

Holy Comforter, come alongside the heavy-laden tonight, and lift off the heaviness that weighs us down. Strengthen us in the inner person, to stand and cry out for the hurting, the sick and the dying.

December 29

Lord, we thank You for Your dogged fidelity in the face of our indifference and rampant ingratitude to Your faithfulness. We are overwhelmed by our limitations and driven to our knees in humility.

December 30

Evening Grace, we're thankful for Your infinite compassion with our brokenness. At the same time, we're enthralled with Your awesome, incomprehensible, and unwieldy mystery of Love and Faithfulness. We can't fully wrap our minds around You. Thanks isn't enough, but it's all we have.

December 31

Your cross, Oh Lord, is the gospel of a crucified Messiah, the might of a King hidden in absurdity and veiled as foolhardiness. From Your cross flows the reality of Your triumph over sin, death, and the Dark Knight. Your crown was made of thorns, Your coronation through crucifixion, and Your reign through resurrection. At the cross, at the cross, where we first received our sight.